Advance praise for Portable Light...

"Be both ordinary & mystic," Mike James advises in a poem from his marvelous new collection, Portable Light. Throughout the book, James takes his own advice to heart. His poems coax ordinary objects and actions to reveal their inmost secrets and ours. From the earliest poems collected here to the latest, James writes with the seeming effortlessness that is the sure mark of a master.

—Howie Good, author of *Famous Long Ago*

Mike James proves himself to be a master of the telling detail, the unexpected phrase that lends a pithy insight or two. His sense of rhythm never falters through these fine selections from a career filled with shifts and twists.

—Raymond Luczak, author of *once upon a twin: poems*

"If I look in the mirror, a few words are written all over my face./Some days it's too much to read them," Mike James says in "You Caught Me Love Dancing," just one of many haunting, deceptively small poems in this collection, which is filled with gorgeous words and big ideas. Riffing on James' recurrent theme of wings as getaway, grace, and salvation, these poems border on noir, and inch toward flight.

—Alexis Rhone Fancher, author of *EROTIC* and poetry editor of *Cultural Daily*

Reading a Mike James poem is like walking into someone else's dream. One has to look for a path through. Once found (and one will find it because James leaves just enough bread crumbs to guide us without telling us how to walk), the landscape reveals itself to be both foreign and familiar. Foreign because his deft navigation in and out of surrealism can leave one shaking and disoriented, yet thrilled at the surprises that emerge from one line to the next. Familiar in that way that all great poetry is familiar: it speaks to the true heart of the human experience. These poems, collected, range from traditional free-verse to prose poems to experimental ghazals. Each poem, regardless of form, is an exploration of Robert Bly's idea of "leaping poetry." James' exploration and re-telling of myth and fable takes us from the narrative we know to completely unexpected places. His cadence, rhythm, and musicality reverberates from each line without blatant pyrotechnics. Instead, James prefers the slow burn that starts with a smoldering whiff of burning leaves that, as the reader spends more and more time inhabiting this sparse yet precise lexicon, builds into a mighty blaze of perfect lines.

—Shawn Pavey, author of *Survival Tips for the Pending Apocalypse*

Previous Collections

Leftover Distances, Luchador, 2021
Double Feature (with John Dorsey), Analog Submissions, 2021
Red Dirt Souvenir Shop, Analog Submissions, 2020
Journeyman's Suitcase, Luchador, 2020
Parades, Alien Buddha, 2019
Jumping Drawbridges in Technicolor, Blue Horse, 2019
First-Hand Accounts from Made-Up Places, Stubborn Mule Press, 2018
Crows in the Jukebox, Bottom Dog, 2017
My Favorite Houseguest, FutureCycle, 2017
Peddler's Blues, Main Street Rag, 2016
The Year We Let the House Fall Down, Aldrich, 2015
Elegy in Reverse, Aldrich, 2014
Past Due Notices: Poems 1991-2011, Main Street Rag, 2012
Shotgun Exchanges, Costmary, 2010
Alternate Endings, Foothills, 2007
Nothing but Love, Pathwise, 2004
Pennies from an Empty Jar, Another Thing, 2002
All Those Goodbyes, Talent House, 2001
Not Here, Green Bean, 2000

PORTABLE LIGHT

New & Selected Poems, 1991–2021

Mike James

Portable Light

Copyright © 2022 by Mike James

Redhawk Publications
The Catawba Valley Community College Press
2550 US Hwy 70 SE
Hickory NC 28602

Robert Canipe, Publisher and Editor-in-Chief
Tim Peeler, Editor
Patty Thompson, Project Coordinator

ISBN: 978-1-952485-47-3

Library of Congress Number: 2021951607

Cover painting by Heather Symmes

All rights reserved, including the right to reproduce this book or portions thereof in any form whatsoever. For information, address the publisher.

For Christopher Harter

Publication Credits

Many of these poems, often in different versions, have appeared in the following journals: *Adirondack Review, Nauseated Drive, Live Nude Poems, River Dog, Deuce Coupe, Shift, Main Street Rag, Black Coffee Review, One, Mad Swirl, Gasconade Review, Heron Clan, As It Ought To Be Magazine, Rye Whiskey Review, Cape Rock, Gargoyle, Rusty Truck, Uppagus, Charlotte Poetry Review, Ted Ate America, Big Muddy, Varnish, Trailer Park Quarterly, Black Coffee Review, Town Creek Poetry, Dead Snakes, I-70 Review, Chiron Review, Skidrow Penthouse, Asheville Poetry Review, Old Red Kimono, Vox Populi, Cultural Daily, Sonic Boom, Verse Virtual, The Artifact, South Florida Poetry Journal, Sanskrit, Homestead Review,* and *Birmingham Poetry Review.*

The selected poems all appeared in previous collections. Thanks to the many editors and publishers who have provided encouragement and support over the years.

Table of Contents

New Poems

A Firefly Letter Across Old China	13
Burnt Up Outside Eden	14
Love & Those Consequences	15
The Invention of Grief	17
Two Rooms	18
Tasting Snowflakes	20
You Caught Me Love Dancing	21
White Bread	22
In This Place	23
Gifts for the Mad Queen	24
"Why Can't You Be Happy Like Everyone Else?"	25
This Always Happens	26
Love Asleep	27
Mandelstam	28
The Train Blows a Whistle. You Can't Whistle	29
Epitaph	30

Selected Poems

Swimmers, Just Married	33
Instructions to the Artist	34
Elegy	36
Mercy	37
The Advancement of Learning	38
Fairy Tales, Fears and the Gymnastics of Love	39
Obituary	40
Postscript, Etc.	41
Homecoming	42
Peddler's Blues	44
Home Remedy	47
Sitting On the Back Porch, In Summer, At Dusk	48

Building a Backyard Fire, Late Winter, Thinking of No One At All	49
Questions for Genesis	50
Theory of Flight	51
On Refusing to Say Grace before Dinner with My Wife	52
Wild Apples	53
Anecdote in a Grassy Field	54
Fragment	55
For Franz Wright	56
The Belt	57
As You Go Along	58
Poem, Mostly Personal	59
Still Life, With Smudges	60
Growing Up, Without Wings	62
Jailbird	64
Listening To an Old Friend Talk, On a Pennsylvania Hillside, Late Autumn	65
Navigating In Place	66
Crow Facts & Variations	67
Marriage Suite	68
My Parents	71
Gertrude Stein	73
Candy Darling	74
Photograph of Delmore Schwartz in Central Park	75
Self-Portrait with Wind and Sky	76
Letter to Jerry Falwell	77
Jack Smith Starter Kit	78
Stan Brakhage	79
Communique	80
Stalin's Icepick	81
On Love Affairs, Break Ups, & Such	82
Just Another Family Reunion	83
This Life	84
Edward, Oh Edward	85
The Brownies of Alice B. Toklas	86
Wounds	87
Traveler's Fable	88
Her Loves	89

Folk Tale without Neon or Blessings	90
The Sundial	91
Samson's Lion	92
Lot's Wife	93
Recipe for Gold	94
A Very Specific Curse	95
The Prisoner	96
The Lottery Ticket in the Mail	97
Is & Not	98
Fallen Angel	99
Pastel Adjustments	100
Steve's in Thailand, so He Claims	101
Uses for Piggy Banks	102
Archaic Landscape without Bubble Bath	103
A Good Day	104
Follow the Ground, Not the Sky	105
Drunk Butterflies near the Missouri River	106
Almost Autumn and Time to Go	107
Falling as We Go	108
Thinning Stars, Along the River	109
Discount Ghazal of Everyday Saints	110
So This Happens	111
Where I'm From	112
Fairy Tale, as Girl was About to Dream	113
Spring Day in the Provinces	114
Hitchhiking Towards the Apocalypse	116
Unfinished Poem	117
The Man in the Yellow Hat	118
So Far Away From Tuscany	119
A Slow, Secret Life	120
Away From the Spotlight, in the July Sun	121
Bright Red Calendar Marks	122
About the Author	123

Portable Light

New Poems

Portable Light

A Firefly Letter Across Old China

after Po Chu-i

I could see to write a letter
If I could fill a lantern with fireflies.

Dark clouds hide a sliver moon.
Tonight's few stars not bright enough
For more than sitting with a cup of wine.

The robe you gave
When you passed through last is one
I wear year-round.
During long summer days it's loose, open.
In the snowy winter, I keep it tight.

A north wind descends from the mountain.
Cools this small valley.

Fishermen sit at the river's edge all day.
Talk about a great orange fish which
Swims through their dreams.

Old friend, there are bridges we won't cross again.
My boat no longer leaves the shore.
Words and words are all I give.

Tonight, fireflies won't light a message.
Tonight, fireflies mark the distances.

Burnt Up Outside Eden

The opposite of your body is what can't be touched.
        This is known best at sixteen in a long summer field.
You hope to kiss every bit of jewelry on the person
        You are with. The moon won't help, out early
In late afternoon blue. The moon's been touched by gloved
        Hands long ago, more than once. More than
Once is a logical progression past one. The most infallible math
        You know involves desire. Desire is a key instead
Of a lock. A matchstick inside a letter. Gasoline in a glass bottle.
        Desire is the ruler beside an open math book.
Measure distance by blessing or by touch. Secrets plus loss plus
        Memory baked in the July sun. In cool grass
We might know burning. The freezing man's last thought is fire.

Love & Those Consequences

I.
Our hands together make a compass.
It points only to
Our bodies.
North and South follow the same line.
We get lost and we get lost.

II.
The Sphinx won't give us a new riddle.
We make do with old ones we didn't solve.
What we know fits on a napkin.
We are working towards road sign simplicity.
Towards wisdom dispatched in a half-smile.

III.
There's no river we don't wish
To swim in.
No body of water we don't
Wish to walk across.
First thoughts, our common bread.

IV.
Already named
There are no pet names
Between us.
We make do with the given.
There is so much.

V.
Some things we don't believe in:
Finger-crossed promises. Block print.
Inside and outside. Common sense.
The yes days. The no days.
Self-taught dance books.

VI.
We ask enough questions
To keep busy.
A vocation of new couples
And three-year-olds.
We are more than. Then some.

VII.
Every looking glass holds our secrets.
They last longer than our smiles.
We count stars in the window
And in the looking glass.
We know the directions of the stars.

The Invention of Grief

There are no closet doors to open to new secrets.
No chests to unlock, then bury in a neighborhood sandbox.

A bed is helpful or, better yet, a couch.
And, of course, a necklace of unsaid things for everyday wear.
And salt if you can find a sharing alchemist.

Also, swallow voices when you sit down to drink.
And each will have a different bitterness.
And each will change the texture of all you know.

Think of moving. Pack your boxes. Throw them away.
Pack ghost boxes. They can be company
For you and all your chairs.

Two Rooms

> *"enter those places"*
> John Wieners

In my dream, I crawl through a window
That connects two rooms. Each looks the same.
Floors, a dull penny copper.
Walls and ceiling, a matching rainy gray.

The window is as you might guess:
Old, wooden, with thick panels of milky glass.
Sometimes, I sit on the windowsill.
One leg in each room.
My toes, feathers just off the ground.

I go out one room into another.
I do this again and again.
It is a game I play while the earth goes round.

There's a door in each room.
I never check for a lock.
Each time I crawl through the window
I'm surprised I'm alone.

More than once I check my skin.
Despite a wish it does not change.
Though my clothes are different
From room to room.

I go out one room into another.
I do this again and again.
It is a game I play while the earth and the sun spin.

The room colors do not change.
No one else comes in.
I never check the doors for a lock.
As I said and said, this is my game.

Tasting Snowflakes

The mayor's daughter smelled like chicken stew and licorice
Every day she had promises and a new suitor
That year it stayed cold through the spring
We ran to keep warm
It was easy to find something to chase us
Our steps were hard
We didn't think of lightness or bird feathers
At the county fair we all watched the shell game
We could never swear we saw a pea
That didn't keep us from guessing

You Caught Me Love Dancing

I like to put my ear to the apartment wall to hear neighbors.
I love when they gossip or share secrets.
Sometimes I only hear mice, their world of gnawing and running.
Sometimes I imagine I hold the wall up.
I keep the building and the universe together, in that order.
After a while, my arms tire.
So I step away, travel from room to room.
I talk to myself, say some of the same words each day.
If I look in the mirror, a few words are written all over my face.
Some days it's too much to read them.

White Bread

When we were out of butter, we dipped dry toast in our coffee.
We never tried to spread and read old coffee grounds.
If a salesman with his dusty brown shoes came to our door,
Smiling with his sample satchel of pretties and wants,
We invited him in.
If he stayed past breakfast, we gave him barn tools to polish.
On the third day he became our cousin.
We taught him to tell time by train whistles.
Winter nights his card tricks kept us entertained.

In This Place

I expect the morning light to end.
And it does.
It does.

The sun reminds me which way is west.
One less thing to guess about.
Take me away from my plowed down routine
I'm mostly lost.

The dreams I wake with don't stay close.
Last night I dreamed about walking among flowers.
This morning, one window frames
The consolation of an empty field.

Gifts for the Mad Queen

Bouquet of coat hangers, sharpened on a brick
Directory of timepieces and lost things
Wreath of hair and twigs, fresh from the river's bottom
Green and gold snake scales for palace-made eye shadow
Cup of salt water for daily pinky baths
Postcard of a silver music box from the country where those are made
Keys to another kingdom, bivouacked on far-away hills

"Why Can't You Be Happy Like Everyone Else?"

because when you hold your breath and pass out, no one comes

because you love the feel of velvet and so few things feel like velvet

because no pigeon ever left a statue to eat from your hand

because every closet you walk into has a wig and a broomstick

because one of the things you do is yourself

because the movies you love are all black and white

because you go on and on

because questions aren't answered, even asked

because sighing is your only exercise

because no one ever invented a love potion that works 365 days

because a damaged *thank you* is the soul of every needle, every pill

because boredom is both habit and mask

because intentions fall away faster than always

because you don't know the combinations for sunlight or bliss

This Always Happens

I start the day walking on eggshells.
My neighbors put them beside my bed at night.
I've tried sleeping with one eye open, but I lose track of when to switch eyes.
I think the neighbors hate that crooning pair of voices in my head.
I don't know how many times someone's yelled for quiet.
One voice sings to a pink glass slipper.
The other voice often cracks, as if gargling with tears.

Love Asleep

after Jorge Guillen

You stretch out your arms in sleep. One hand brushes
Against my shoulder. Surprises my insomnia.
The window's moon is a barren companion.
Your sleep is often restless, but lasts through the darkness.
So many nights I watch your face.
Imagine where the boat of night takes you.
Every morning, you tell me about last night's dreams.
There's always an envelope of images
Fresh from that other country.

Mandelstam

Crumbs beside the kitchen table
Don't lead through the forest
Those were other days

That fairy tale started with hunger
Hunger, a white pebble in a worn leather shoe
Every witch knows how to sharpen a pebble

Some witches keep their power beyond one life
They linger in morning mist when it lingers too long
No one can be trusted

The forest stays through every season
The forest stays through every season
Repetition, that spell we learn as children

The tree line, a green door
With dreams on both sides

The Train Blows a Whistle. You Can't Whistle

Some people burn empty houses just to watch the sparks. Old pine has a special scent like some soaps and carpet cleaners and a very few aftershaves. You spend your days looking for a comfortable place to sit. Every bird bath holds something other than water. There was that fainting couch you dreamed of as a child. Afternoons of glue sticks and glitter. Snorting glitter was never a good idea, but so many bad ideas lead to the purest joy. You were never a child who could draw a tree even when you were sitting on a limb.

Epitaph

He used old stilettos to plant his garden. It was really just an
Onion patch. Mouthwash, aftershave, perfume, and flowered
Ointments hid the smell of his favorite food. As his doormat said,
What's a Fellow to Do? Success came with everything not
Related to anything. Outside of money, love affairs, traffic tickets,
Beauty supplies, and portion control, his life was charmed.
He held a record for most Pythagoras quotes used when
Ordering a bloody Mary. Friends gave him books on the Queen.
Maybe that's why he called butter knives daggers.
No matter, he never complained about bite marks or potluck.
His favorite food was hillbilly porridge. His favorite game was
Glory hole peek-a-boo. His laugh could be heard three stoplights
Over. Did I mention he couldn't whisper? Or say the alphabet
While you watched? He never offered a cold shoulder to the world.

Selected Poems

Portable Light

Swimmers, Just Married

we swim and find our bodies full length

wine drunk, we are interrupted
when a catfish jumps near us   we laugh

our mouths take in the wet moon
fallen upon the water

so many days without rain   the lake low
the water still clear

days without anger   the sleep-smile
of the first married

this is the beginning to all fairy tales
all we ever learn

Instructions to the Artist

> *"Nothing is gained by assurance."*
> Ted Berrigan

Get a dog that is friendlier than people…
    feed him bacon scraps &
      tell him your worst jokes.

Have a head that is harder than the shitheads
    that surround you.

Buy all your books second hand.

Buy a plant…a cactus, preferably, or a loving fern.

Be like Bukowski & drink almost anything.

Rent a house with many windows.

Be like St. Francis & drink only water.

Count out the steps to the closest source of light.

Save all the letters you receive, let them be a constant,
    a journal of all that you know.

Read the comics while in the bathtub.

Be both ordinary & mystic.

Think, when you are walking, about how your legs feel…
    study the ease of a lazy man.

Live by eating leftovers from the refrigerators of friends.

Elegy

i spent part
of today

trying to remember
the taste

of coffee in my
father's house

the way it was
strong from

the four scoops
of off-brand

and how the
water held

the brackish taste
of copper

from the old pipes
fed by the well

Mercy

when you say
mercy
hold the word in your mouth
a moment

the weight is the weight
of a thousand pebbles
placed
one at a time
on your tongue

if you feel dizzy
let your hands
fall to
your sides

the birds
that gather darkness
may come
to rest there

The Advancement of Learning

i don't regret
any time
i've spent
staring out the window

nothing good
was ever learned
in a hurry

olson says

the simplest
things
      are always
last

the years it took
to learn to fish

to bait a hook
the proper
way

Fairy Tales, Fears and the Gymnastics of Love

in any fairy tale a large bird can say
beware of this and that

as someone who
often listens to large, talking birds
i am often afraid

the dark does not scare me
and snakes have never
occupied
even one of my dreams

but frogs-even the tiny tree frog-
make me sweat
worse than long distance running

also, i don't like flight attendants

i am not afraid of them
but i don't like them and that
has not been said enough
in poems

instead, we say that you are beautiful
or a beautiful fool

we give these two refrains
a million variations

as if we could not stand on our heads
and think
of anything else to say

Obituary

say nice things about me   jack said

tell everyone that i loved
black olives
sinclair lewis and the early work of
philip guston

my secrets were numerous and
avowedly profane

only once in my life did i quote
rick flair
(the greatest wrestler of all time)

the quote is in greek
and untranslatable

tell people i always said
what i thought
          i never danced around a subject
like a bird around a tree

that's not true, but it is how
i would like to be remembered

surely, you can see that

Postscript, Etc.

at night we shared our insomnia
over the phone

neither watched our words
nor counted the time

he told me
       he got eight hours' sleep
an hour or two
here and there

with no "real job"
he made do

sold books and antiques

ghost wrote articles

worked a town fair, once,
as a ticket man

mainly, he drank coffee
and smoked hand-rolled cigarettes

mainly, he talked
and talked

his whole life filled with words
with what he meant to say

as there's always something else
as there's always one more thing

Homecoming

> *"No dog knows my smell."*
> Robert Lowell

pulpwood had its way here

what land hasn't been clear cut
is a county away

the town gave up fixing roads
six years ago

potholes are the new industry

relatives no longer ask
when you'll move back

instead, they ask about
other places
curse you in their prayers

at a gas station
an old teacher doesn't
remember you
your voice or any charm
you imagined

she treats you like the stranger
you are

when the last mill closed
the town
should have had a party

with fireworks, speeches
and confetti like dreams

Peddler's Blues

a beggar
offers thanks
perhaps a
blessing if
that's his caste

a peddler
sells what he
can (cheap wares
throughout the
county or
town) one poor
neighbor to
another

my father
told me the
difference
when i was
seven and
he quit the
mill to work
from his old,
oil-drinking,
blue ford van

i'm it, son
my own boss
it's all me

those phrases

with either
laugh or frown
reflecting
that day's luck

after school
i rode with
him (never
doubted my
fortune) knocked
door to door
to gather
customers
see what could
be had for
a good price

he set shop
opened van
side door to
advertise
apples, sweet
potatoes,
oranges, grape
fruits, candy,
watermelons,
watches, toys,
jewelry and
general
merchandise

everyone
seemed to want
at least a

Portable Light

bit of what
he had…but

on credit
which, after
a while, he
gave and gave
(though it's not
selling if
no one pays)

when his van,
at last, quit
his old boss
at the old
mill welcomed
him back…but
for night shift…
a penance
dad called it
for leaving

sometimes he'd
mention that
greek who flew
near the sun
say wings are
made for use
if you fly
go far, long

Home Remedy

mix dew wet cobwebs
with clotted, white flour

apply to scar
while whispering
loved one's name

Sitting On the Back Porch, In Summer, At Dusk

my children play in the neighbor's field
games they make up themselves

my wife somewhere else
wherever that is

suddenly, a crow lands
on the other side of the porch

fresh from our fig tree and the near darkness
closer than crows normally get

we give each other good long stares

after a few minutes he makes his loud cry
then flies away

i can't repeat the cry he makes
only the silence he leaves

Building a Backyard Fire, Late Winter, Thinking of No One At All

my backyard fire pit hand dug, uneven,
cemented with yard rocks, re-used brick

the only skills my hands know
are ones money's lack teaches

no snow or frost though still a chill
what better time to build a fire

there's dried-out pine, scrub bush,
castoff lumber from the vacant lot next door

there's a box of matches, another of wine,
a chair and a red, wool blanket too

if my neighbor drops by we'll toast
from my box or her bottle

her last husband gone to somewhere else
since last september

the stars out in a few minutes
as of now, the sky's still blue

Questions for Genesis

did eve's lips
grow lustful
after the first
bite of the
apple did she
inhale in
anticipation
of adam's
scent think
of her own
which she
barely knew
did she
quickly look
over each
shoulder to
see if animals
saw her
different
before she
chewed

Theory of Flight

you walk every field for miles

never see a bush burn with
more than autumn

the sky follows you
like a habit

you try to be invisible
that never works

so you pick up every shiny rock
to wish on

the paint by numbers kit
you want for your life
never arrives

so you look for treasure
in roadside hub caps

you look for faces
in the tarnish
of wrinkled leaves

there's no cocoon
you won't crawl inside

beneath your jacket are dark wings

On Refusing to Say Grace before Dinner with My Wife

i don't know what to make
of the language
of grace

those words
don't cling to me
the way a blanket does
on mid-winter
mornings

or the way we cling
to one another
at night
as we swim
across the ocean of our bodies
past the edge of our wants

the night sky full of stars
mariners used
for passage
their breath filling sails
with a word
that can be a taunt
a promise
or something close to grace

home

Wild Apples

so, here i am gathering apples
behind a neighbor's foreclosed house

andy and lauren moved away last year
the house, bank owned and empty since

over the years, this tree grew (untended,
accidental) in the corner of their acre lot

in the part of the yard they left
to weeds and shrubs and never cut

it takes at least eight years to grow a tree
so full of knotty, spotted, sour green apples

my grandfather called these horse apples
they grew wild in pastures he once knew

the fattest ones are the highest, near the sun
no horse could reach those

with my ladder and a paper grocery bag
i'll get enough for two pies

one for me and another for a neighbor
out of work, but still in her house

since sometimes dessert comes before the meal
as grace can come in the harvest of wild things

Anecdote in a Grassy Field

once
my old man saw a stone
suddenly decide to be a bird

the stone sprouted wings and a beak
in a quick, blinking instant
flew straight up from the ground
then away

it circled back
twice
never came down close enough
for him to catch

after a while
the stone flew past distant trees
out of sight
the whir of wings a memory

this happened more than a while back
before i was born
when miracles still took place

Fragment

after Bill Knott

because always, always at least one couple is fighting
somewhere down a road or street
because they are mostly saying grievances
months, maybe years, old
patience, that long-winded virtue, sometimes gives up
after a last attempt to lecture into love, into submission

For Franz Wright

      d. 5-14-2015

if you carried words
in a tin cup
some sparrow
would
come along
think they were
bread crumbs

you'd stand
in place
say a blessing
as he ate
the words you had left

until your body hurt
so you wished
it was no
longer yours

until your heart, quite naturally,
blossomed into wings

The Belt

some nights, mill tired or drunk with
payday laughter, he never touched it

so it hung on a wall nail
a skinned snake done striking

there was never a full week though
when his grip didn't feel that cracked, black leather

when a *goddam* didn't preface
the clear wisp of breaking air

a small bird, i knew little
except the sky and one tree

still, i knew when it was all over
and every tear had left the river of my body

he would gather me from the floor
into the dark, hairy nest of his arms

hold me chest close
say, *it's alright boy, it's alright*

as he tried to whisper light
back into my eyes

As You Go Along

for Mbembe Milton Smith

say you make your living writing poems
that will get
people talking

let everyone know you need a bigger apartment
not only for all your books
but also for the pet goat used as a paper shredder

mention how your words come as dictation
from a muse who hides, like a prize, in your cereal box

talk about gold teeth as a retirement plan
and polka dots as the pattern
of the future

a beard and sunglasses are not bad for aesthetics
but nothing stands out
like an eye patch
and a willingness to speak like a pirate, now and then

before they take you to a quiet room
in a special hospital
for people just like you
try walking on water for at least a day

Poem, Mostly Personal

i like surprises
and not just the sexual kind
either

like the time
you walked down the steps
wearing only
flip-flops
and a tuba

no, i like surprises
in general

that sudden intake
of breath

the recognition
of how the world changes
instantly
before us

the way we felt
that year in the north
when snow fell
during the richness
of summer

every red rose
dipped in
white

Still Life, With Smudges

after tasting
one long
finger
fresh from
the yellow sun
batter of
a cake
or ladling
up the
winter taste
of venison
in stew
my grandmother
might pause
to say

close enough
is enough

then add
two seconds
later

perfection's
like that
little boy
who won't
get dirty
who won't
play rough

Growing Up Without Wings

her mother told her

fear any man
whose voice
grows louder in the dark
he is not the one
to marry

but if
for too many days
the brown of his eyes reminds you
of a forest
to hide in

if saying yes ever seems
not only
the easiest
but
the only path

then keep your voice down
on the phone

learn to keep quiet secrets

also
keep a few dollars
hidden
maybe wrapped in an old sweater's wool warmth
maybe in an empty makeup case
places a man will never search
will never think to

keep at least
one friend
from before your marriage
who knows you
by your scraped knee stories
by the deep chest sounds of your laugh
this friend will be
an island
in a river that changes course

more than all this
remember
even if you pray and pray nightly
with full belief and unfisted heart
prayer only works
outside the reach of his arms

Jailbird

some people belong in prison
my mother
said
about my father
who after fifty two years on earth
left behind
three milk crates of possessions
and a rented room
high cherokee cheekbones
a love of white wine and the old testament
and a dance called the "prison shuffle"
mom would
never do

sit down
she would say
when i tried to get her
to dance

when i was with your father
i had enough dancing
to do me
until cows or jesus
came home

she always
laughed
when she said that
as if she were saying it
for the first time

Listening To an Old Friend Talk, On a Pennsylvania Hillside, Late Autumn

I.

the wind on the hill grass
same as the wind on the river
same as the wind in my hair grown long with the season

the wind surprises us
seems to come from nowhere
across field, water, and sky

middle age and old age, both surprise us
along a dirt path, suddenly, a vast rock pile of years

II.

i've forgotten some of my words
some of the long, precise, melodious ones
used for crossword puzzles
not for singing

i can only speak simply now
i can make little comments about the weather

winter is coming
the air already settling with a chill

winter is more than a season

Navigating In Place

we are always looking down

true, above us, clouds take the shape we wish
and there seems no end to the sky's depth of blue

but it's what's right beneath our feet
that holds attention

we find a rock, a piece of trash, a bone-shaped stick
we can't look away from

we fall in love with the misshapen, with cast off things
we build a life from the architecture of debris

our stories start in the dirt and go up or down from there
this is even true of the fairy tales where every creature has wings

Crow Facts & Variations

if god were a crow
the world would spin in the black pearl of her eyes

the world would spin and spin
black would be the color to measure others by

***

if crows could reach the stars
they would

they'd have new worlds to scavenge among

crows are scavengers
(read survivors)

crows make do

***

a field crow calls out in that broken voice
not even a crow mother loves

no one answers
so there's silence, which is an answer

crows can nest in silence
if they must

they can stay there as long as the world can

Marriage Suite

i can make nothing
with my hands

have learned
no craft
of wood, needle
or stone

am often wrong on
measurements

all i know of
geometry
comes from studying
the lines
of your face

***

some things i know
only from
you

are true because
you said them

whole world might
say otherwise

***

i watch your hands
in the quiet canyon of your sleep

there are dreams you
follow
again and again

they are the stories you tell
on waking

***

dreams are the second-best thing
you always
say

you've always said

***

after these many years
memory takes up
more space

once, it used just a closet
now, it demands a whole floor

***

that first, rented house
with barely a bed and table

one neighbor came
with green apples
and water
in a clear, glass jar

she sat with us
told us
how it was
before we came

My Parents

1.

the horizon is my father
back from the sea
      his eyes
shallow blue

they are blue
because i see them, know they are blue
they are blue because
he tells me his eyes are what people
(read women/girls)
notice first

      beach sky blue
      vacation blue
      dixie-land trumpet blue
      not blue like *the blues*
      blue with no shadow sadness

2.

my mother left one day
in her small, white car
to get groceries

never came back

her eyes
almost green
      (red in the corners)

        when she squinted
        they took the shape of wings

Gertrude Stein

Picasso said she would grow into the portrait he painted. And she did. All the rounded spaces she filled in. Her eyes held a place in the distance and after a while she was at that place. It did not happen quickly. It took many years. The earth turned round and round and the place came to her at last. It happened while she sat steady in her chair and sure of herself. The place was filled with flowers.

Candy Darling

Sometimes the best looking women are men. Because anyone can be beautiful or at least have beautiful hair. If your name is James it doesn't have to be. If your hair is brown it doesn't have to stay that way. There are a thousand different people within each person. And that's just in one week.

Photograph of Delmore Schwartz in Central Park

The eyes are tired from looking inward. (He hasn't slept since
he was a small boy playing baseball in a vacant lot. Back then,
the dreams were not of Marx, Mann or Joyce, but of his laughing
father.) In conversation, he leans on cigarettes as though each is a
cane. So there are three mountains he climbs: boredom, alienation,
and illness. Each gets steeper with every ascent. His steps add
to his weight. He is always cold. Even in a New York August,
he wears scarf and coat. He looks as though he is thinking as he
always is. Beside him on the bench, his pretzel lunch sits and sits.

Self-Portrait with Wind and Sky

Give me a field of pristine grass, untouched by man and I'll lose interest before the next sentence. Put in a few boot tracks, tire marks, even an old beer can, and I'll perk up, start looking for people I know. Friends. Relatives. Friends of relatives. Friends of friends. Maybe that old girlfriend who always wanted sex when there were no buildings around. Let me walk the grass. I might identify the three birds and four insects I learned, on a field trip, in fifth grade. I might start to misspeak. Call the open sky my cathedral. Find a mossy ditch to crawl in and pray.

Letter to Jerry Falwell

Once, walking the streets of Lynchburg, VA, almost close enough to the university to hear students praying to sky, I saw a man playing a toy piano on the sidewalk. He sat on a tiny stool in front of it, not smiling at all, dressed in a three-piece suit of a style and birthmark thirty years older.

I went to a diner, there on Main Street. Had my burger and beer lunch.

The diner served home-cut fries and advice. The fries were large, finger width. The advice was in whispers.

No one mentioned the man out front on the toy piano. Maybe that's a common occurrence in Lynchburg where miracles are an expectation.

Jack Smith Starter Kit

Be brilliant even in your dreams. Dress like a hustler or a beauty pageant winner or a fry cook, dependent on your mood. Your mood will guide you as much as your brilliance. Use great titles as bookmarks for projects left unfinished in the air or on the floor. Give up all thoughts of money or nice teeth. Perfect smiles are over-rated and a twentieth century invention. Stud your vocabulary with words from trailer parks, gangster films, and symbolist poets. Build a shrine to personal masterpieces. Never leave your gas can and matches at home.

Stan Brakhage

What's out of focus stays that way. Call it abstraction. Though it's really movement. The blur is something happening. It's life without clean lines.

Show a hand shuffling a deck of cards. Not two hands. One. Show another hand with a cheap engagement ring and green painted nails. Let that hand draw a card. Someone can say a few words or not.

Communique

for Chase Dimock

Bosnian snipers are everywhere. Especially in the wheat fields outside of Omaha. They send obscene postcards to the local police department and to the many chapters of the DAR. They make prank phone calls, in southern accents, to retirement homes for Union soldiers. Almost every bridge underpass is riddled with their secret graffiti, so easily translated with a basic decoder ring. Some graffiti give directions to heaven. Others, only directions to home.

Stalin's Icepick

The first time Stalin saw Trotsky, he was struck by the way he held a teacup. The way his fingers seemed to gather warmth in the open cathedrals that were his hands. He wondered if Trotsky's goatee ever bathed in milk, if his eyes ever slowed from dancing.

Stalin often thought of Trotsky at night. He would smoke his pipe and play with his favorite icepick, the one with a handle engraved with a fist holding a flower with a small bee in the center.

On Love Affairs, Break Ups, & Such

Heart plus flowers equals a drug store valentine. Open the card. There's a door inside. Behind the door, a tunnel goes down farther than light shows. Don't be afraid of the dark. Tell yourself that again and again, like an old man in an ancient church saying thankless prayers. Go on in. Delight in the cold. Your hunger comes in waves, directed by the moon. It ebbs and flows.

Just Another Family Reunion

My sisters and I argue over who is the biggest disappointment. My parents say it's a tie. When we play cards we bet mistakes. I'll see your DUI and raise you a divorce. I'll add a divorce to yours and throw in a bankruptcy. This is how it is whenever we get together. Our kids play or else beat each other until their faces resemble bruised tomatoes. Our father sits on the couch and dreams of a better remote. In the kitchen our mother adds tears to the soup she's been cooking all these years.

This Life

Yesterday a half-built mansion open to rain, raccoons, and a few young, stray vandals. Today a hunter's shack, cold in the woods, where shadows gather around a ghost fire. Tomorrow's foundation rocks scattered across a damp, distant field of knife-like weeds, grey blooming flowers.

Edward, Oh Edward

Gave up dreaming because he could. Decided to cloud watch instead. He really wanted to go to Rome and cloud watch there. He heard Rome has the oldest clouds. Cloud watching is like coloring without crayons. When he was kid, he never had crayons. All he had was clouds and dreams and a pet monkey named Gilgamesh who walked with him when he took a walk and fed pigeons with him in the park. He loved Gilgamesh until he ran away to a circus. That's always the risk. Even his mother said that.

The Brownies of Alice B. Toklas

Some women have small thin mustaches, pepper black, soft as a blanket worn to over-ripe thread. The mustache might be softer than the face it decorates, which might be all points and slopes. Descriptive enough? Gertrude says, description is not literature. If you only wish to see what others see you can only look at color photographs. Never at words. Even road signs read differently depending on where you are going, where you have been, if it is raining, and if the sun is shining through the rain. The sign might be on a street in Oakland, California, which always seems distant even if you are only one city over. As places go it is just as good as any other place, certainly no better.

Wounds

Every wound made him more invisible. One by one, they accumulated. Sometimes paper cut small. Other times big as a toe, a foot, a leg. There was the divorce that cost him the house, the car, the cat, and a little more than half his heart. The job that called him too old and let him go and go. And the friend who took a trip past the end of the road. Each erased a little more. Until the morning when the bathroom mirror barely held a face to shave.

Traveler's Fable

A hotel, sick of ins and outs and noise complaints and made up stories at the hotel bar. Yes, a hotel sick of laundered sheets and room service and little scented soap bars and muffled one night stands. This hotel dreamed itself into a lunchbox, carried by a man at the mill. Opened and shut only a few times each day. There only for him. A thermos, the best company. The thermos once a lighthouse, years before.

Her Loves

She loved corsets and dictionaries and various definitions of both. She liked to read her different dictionaries while wearing different corsets. She often did this while drinking herbal tea. She didn't really like tea, but was convinced of its goodness for her and her figure. No one could convince her otherwise. Even the medical librarian who came, daily, to brush sparks from the dark embers of her hair, and to charm with mouthfuls of polysyllables, even he could not.

Folk Tale without Neon or Blessings

for Shawn Pavey

God was tired, so she took the day off. She was sick of panic and endless needs. Sick of that old scale of wants versus thanks. Couldn't fathom another roundabout day of angels gossiping over people whose magic scars they guessed at.

So, after yoga and a garden walk, she carved for hours on a rock she couldn't lift and studiously didn't think of kids. Late in the day, in dust white work clothes, with wind blowing just enough to lighten green on grass and leaves, she sat and sipped her tea and wondered how anything she ever made could still exist.

The Sundial

Scissors, sick of any line not completely straight, chased Circle out of the house and locked the door. Circle, though, knew how to make friends and quickly did.

All around Circle stones of similar size gathered, a dozen in all, to hear of life inside the house and to hear of the way all shapes came to be. Except on very dark, cloudy days this became the routine.

Samson's Lion

When he came back to look at the bee-riddled carcass, it was to mourn. After many months, parts of the desert worn hide still shimmered. If the lion had not sprung quickly off a shining rock, had not bared teeth and claws with intention, he never would have struck. He loved most animals more than most men.

The honey he found surprised him, by its place, its abundance, by the sweetness the bees gathered and gathered. He brushed aside the bees. Gave no notice to stings. He sat in the dirt, amid sun and rock, dry bones and honey. So filled with joy at the surprise of a desert feast, he let honey drip from his mouth and beard.

Lot's Wife

The marriage was never good. Lot lived and lectured within the dull walls of his piety. Never sipped water or ate a crust of bread without giving thanks so all might hear. In Sodom, his eyes watched the ground. When women stood in doorways and called and called he did not answer. Instead, he scurried down the one path to home. At night his sand-coarse hands touched his wife: the same spots in the same order. He knew only one way to enter the house of her body…quickly, while shuddering thanks. Beneath him, she dreamed of another's salt. Her whole life, a backward glance.

Recipe for Gold

- ❖ Burn a matchstick down to a thumbnail ember
- ❖ Crush the ember in an antique crucible, borrowed from a retired alchemist
- ❖ Add salt, but no more than a dove can carry on its smallest feather
- ❖ Toss in three red rose petals, moist with desire's blessings
- ❖ Wrap a black silk string, twice, around the crucible
- ❖ Close your eyes and sit with an unblended heart
- ❖ In all of this, never once think of dirt, water, or sky
- ❖ Results depend on soul purity, local miracle frequency

A Very Specific Curse

May grammar make a tight leash around you. Babel descend on your tongue. Your dentures slip into whistles. Those whistles your only music as you are called to dance, dance. And you learn love can be flammable as you forget every star you ever thought to touch.

The Prisoner

"One of the prisoners had not seen the stars for 22 years."
New York Times

That night, when he walked outside, he thought he was living in memory. A boy, camping, the year before his father died. No tent, but four blankets and a fire. The stars all made of fire. Too far for night warmth. All of them at the edge of where darkness starts and ends.

The Lottery Ticket in the Mail

for Scott Wannberg

Wasn't a winner. No one likes me that much. No return address on the envelope. The ticket purchased the year of my birth. Someone's sending a message I can't guess.

I'll put it on the refrigerator right beside the love notes from Noam Chomsky, the death threats from each of the last three popes, and the apple pie recipe my mother sent right before she disinherited me and married a margarita. My refrigerator door is a collage of disappointments. If I ever opened it, I might sob into a river I couldn't cross.

I've given up keeping flowers in the kitchen. It's no fun being a fan of anything that quickly dies. Just ask the man who keeps fruit flies as pets. He spends half of each day weeping.

Is & Not

There are so many things Mike is not. Like not especially tall. Like that. More things he is not than things he is. Not black, brown, or tan. Not female, though possessed of feet and hands quite feminine. Not anyone other than a person named Mike. No nicknames. No aliases. Someone who often speaks in couplets and says *fuck* a lot. Who says fuck more than he does fuck, which is the most people way. Those named Mike. Those named Larry. Those named Leslie. Those named Heather. Those who read Edward Dahlberg with one eye shut. Those who file away old postcards as if memory is an unchanging place. People awash in prepositions *of, for*, *despite, without*.

Fallen Angel

The first job he took, after he quit Heaven, was at a butcher shop. His halo sliced meat pretty well. The shop owner liked the novelty, as did customers used to nothing more interesting than sausage plumpness. But, like even the best Broadway performance, the gig ended. The health department sent him out the door, amid the owner's sobs and sighs. Halos are hard to clean, no matter how strong the disinfectant. Slicing with one violates regulations which date back before phone book popularity.

After the butcher shop, he became a cowboy. He tied a rope to his halo and called it a lasso. It worked almost as well as Wonder Woman's golden lasso. Though she was from a different place.

Pastel Adjustments

His life, a vending machine filled only with Zagnuts. He was tired of sameness. What he really wanted was a faux leather knapsack of absurdities. Not for any commonly misspelled tattoos or a not so lackadaisical snowflake. More an unhatched egg flying in perfect geometry across the sky or even wind blowing both ways at once. He had a fondness for anything not seen. He didn't always drive through ghosts on his way to work. Though on any morning he might recall the red of Sally Hedgepath's nail polish. Anything long remembered becomes something else. As a kid, he liked to juggle. His mother told him stop that, go outside and hit a ball. And so he ran and ran like Dick and Jane and Spot. He learned to speak in simple sentences. All his socks were black. When he found a penny he picked it up. When he had enough pennies he rolled them. He never put a red or pink ribbon on his penny rolls before he took them to the bank, but he thought about it more than a few times.

Steve's in Thailand, so He Claims

It's really impolite to smoke in a rickshaw so he eats peanuts instead and has that Vogue daydream about red flare pants. The daydream's been in reruns so long he knows every runway turn. Still, like the ride, it goes on. He knows what he likes and doesn't mind. Yesterday was more fun than today even if one or two old scars blossomed red, raw again. Some gardens grow no matter how little we tend. The traffic immense and almost post card framed. The driver declines a peanut offer. His manners, professional and intense. The peanuts are unsalted, so there's that.

Uses for Piggy Banks

When they are not pink they still seem to think pink thoughts. Projection doesn't make that less true. There's no practical use for pink like there is for money. Think pink house in a yellow field, no tree or neighbor in sight. Farmers are practical and must be. Maybe this one loves pigs and flamingos.

Money is a kind of poetry, Wally said. And that doesn't rhyme, the young girl replied. Change rhymes with game or nearly so.

The empty pig makes no sound. Then there's the rattle of coins sliding in. One by one. Large and small. Small and small. The child makes a game of this. She chants a nonsense rhyme with the rattle. She never names the game.

Archaic Landscape without Bubble Bath

Whenever he had bad dreams, he realized he had watched the news. Stuffed animals, graham crackers, plastic water bottles, and baby dolls were all in cages. The cage wire looked like sand paper. Desert sand speckled the wire throughout night and day. So at least sand and wind still worked together. The stuffed animals held the most color. The air was dry and dryer. And, of course, the sky lacked rain. So nothing bloomed on plains or hills. The clouds went west or south or stayed in the north. After a while no one thought to look at the sky.

A Good Day

That game where we pretend to be strangers and get married anyway. I think it's called Paradox Heaven. Normally, it ends in a draw. Most days, we try to be angels though it's hard not to curse in our prayers. Neither of us has a pedigree longer than a postage stamp. Family history is mainly a secret no one wants to share. On days when we don't shoot stop signs we like to research circuses to run away to. Elephant riding is something we might enjoy. Like good cowboys we practice our gallop on broomsticks. If we don't get splinters, we call it a good day.

Follow the Ground, Not the Sky

If I know where I'm going, I don't get there faster.
My pace doesn't change. I'm slow, unsteady.
I can follow the sun, like on a mission, and still lose my way.

My past makes a trail I circle back to. Often, I meet an old self.
Normally, look away. My satchel, stuffed with unsaid things,
Gets heavier and heavier.

Thunderstorms tell me the Devil is real. Lightning reminds me
To shut my eyes. Sometimes, I count or hold my breath.
Sometimes, I play pretend.

I never gave the Devil up. He's always around the next corner
Or ready to steal my shadow if I turn away.
He carries the long list of my fears.

In a way, the Devil is my oldest friend. If that sounds sad, it is.
There's never been an angel on my shoulder. Not once.
And my shoulders are thin.

Drunk Butterflies near the Missouri River

for Jason Ryberg

"nothing but your blind, stupefied heart"
John Thompson

Lord, even without belief, today is enough. A little chant
I say to myself. Structured right, it is a hymn.
Not even I like to hear my singing.

Yesterday, I almost got lost going home. I wasn't following
The advice of every teacher: Pay attention!
I got through school. Got home.

I drive when I'm lonely. Take a lot of back, dirt roads.
Never found a collapsed bridge in any river. My luck.
That's what keeps me driving.

It's August. Heat takes up everything. I think of weather.
Think of rain. Nothing changes. It's still August.
With or without the river.

I've always lived beside a river. Never once hopped
Across on rocks. I distrust currents. Don't like darkness moving
Fast or slow. Will walk a long way to take a good bridge.

I've heard every cliché about home is true. I'll say that,
Smile stupidly. I don't always watch how hard the wind blows.
I keep going. I go.

Almost Autumn and Time to Go

> *"exhausted from saying goodbye"*
> Shawn Pavey

Jesus didn't say much. Hard to speak when your words come out
Unsavory red. People ask and ask. How many answers
Are a head shake or a long stare?

The tongue shapes the world as best it can. Tell me what
I don't know. A long list. Start with a's. Vowels carry us along,
Not always merrily. Our tongues click and cluck.

We say please to the fishhook when hungry. Please to the needle
When sick. Easy to forget the niceties. Hear that preacher curse
When he falls in the dark.

Neighbors don't hear us. We don't listen to ourselves.
Maybe we do and don't care. Is that a conundrum, like:
When is near far and far near? Almost never, unless it is.

Everything goes back to travel. Get to heaven or just over there.
Some of us stay ready. We live by love or fear.
Maybe adventures are one street over. Maybe streets are empty.

The answer to travel is always not here. Grace might be
In the very next town. There might be room to spare.
Sift along long enough, a few things get clear.

Falling as We Go

> *"uneasy at last"*
>   John Berryman

You go swimming with a smooth stone on your back.
Heavy, but fits well. Maybe call the stone, wants.
Better yet, at your midpoint, call it, years.

What do you give up in middle-age? Desire? No.
It lingers and won't leave. It is a stain that stays.
Or a knife kept loose in a sheath. An uncertain blade.

We take smaller steps as we age. Pretend that's a dance.
In a way it is. Two steps forward. One step back.
That's a shuffle habit makes.

Curse the night. It doesn't change. The moon's half-dollar
Remains unspent. The dark gives cheap cover for want.
Ask Old Man Lot. It was always like this.

Your hands tell what's real. True when young and now.
Gravity no longer a friend. If you fall, you find what's near.
Sometimes you call out. Sometimes you keep still

Thinning Stars, Along the River

> *"Heaven goes on without us."*
> John Thompson

We feed ourselves river oysters. Try to find an old man's face
Lining any inner shell. Dinner is an art project.
And a drinking contest. A time to argue, loudly. An excuse.

Stuck with our change jars and our poor, back-of-the
Gas station penny tosses. Still here, with barely a name.
There's no well big enough for all our wishes.

Our mythologies made from childhood, broken hearts,
Nightmares, and game shows. No master key for the myths.
Each suffers the calendar, warms or cools with seasons.

At night we check the sky. Find the Big Dipper. Find the Little
Dipper. Give up then. The sky is something we can drink from.
Often, we can't believe how polished it is.

No crow will ever carry a star across the sky. There's a myth
If you want to make it. Even with a well-lit moon, some things
Stay hidden. Darkness is never clean or clear.

Discount Ghazal of Everyday Saints

We might forage for back door secrets and elevator shoes.
Decorate our houses in flea market drapery to resemble
A penny arcade. It's all done for emphasis.

Sometimes we wish we stayed as we were born: naked,
Careless of fat lines. Some of us age into palm readers
And call our fingerprints our greatest gifts.

Once, I knew a man who claimed he was double-crossed
By angels and garbage men. Every whisper resembled
A yell. Despite it all, his mouth was framed by smile lines.

My town is known for orphanages, plus street corners
Occupied by sword swallowers. The last circus left months ago.
Go by the unemployment office. There's always a line.

Most of my friends live with hallucinations. Reality is where
They put their emphasis. When we all gather we count gifts,
Naked or draped in the curtains of Scarlet O'Hara.

So This Happens

If I believed in sunrises as a cure all for late night disagreements,
I'd wake you early and call you to an eastern window.
The two of us have almost outlived belief.

Rumi started out offering knowledge to any stranger in his path.
He ended offering blessings. Is that how we change
Between morning and night?

One of the things I like about you is how you make halos
Seem like an affectation of angels and rock stars.

Your best friend says your eyes are blue. I always thought
They were harvest green…the color of my favorite,
Flea market-bought, t-shirt.

Some people don't like to get dirty. Others swan dive into any
Trash bin. You are in the middle register. One note either way.

I do everything quickly, even rush my love and anger.
You take your time, set up house.
I look over every fence, make up stories as I pass.

After all these years we ask the same questions again and, yes,
Again. An old test answered in pencil. We ask…
Which blank do you fill in?

Where I'm From

On one side of the river, it always rains
Half the men are named Noah
The sky is a wet pillow

The other side of the river is filled with ne'er-do-well cousins
They are tan from six-days-a-week sunshine
The dress code is hand-me-down suits, boutonniere

Men still fish both sides of the river
No one has caught a fish in a hundred years
Once a month people gather to walk across the water
My grandmother said this started before her mother was a girl

Fairy Tale, as a Girl was About to Dream

Brown fox flees storybook
Brown fox runs
Brown fox runs
Running is a way for brown fox
Brown fox's shadow also runs, has a tail
Brown fox's shadow has no scent
Brown fox's fur smells of burnt leaves
Some fire is always burning
Brown fox always finds a fire
Fires burn trails
Ash scent is strong and stays
Embers glow even on starless nights
Brown fox still runs on starless nights
Brown fox runs
Dark birds trill in holes of absent stars

Spring Day in the Provinces

for Jeff Gundy

"I have hardened my heart only a little."
                              Robinson Jeffers

The first day warm enough for my favorite Hawaiian shirt, without goosebumps.

The fabric, faded and thin. Before I put it on, I check for holes.

Fresh deer tracks beside the mailbox this morning. No time of day I can't hear the interstate's rumblings.

The former governor just said he supports the President, no matter what he does.

If I stop and listen close I hear baby birds crying for worms or warmth in their nest above a back porch column. The father, blue-headed. The mother, all gray. They take turns.

Everything is already green: grass, weeds, trees, and ivy.

A foreign leader stated, "The diversity of our country is actually one of our greatest strengths and a source of tremendous resilience and pride." The White House, surprisingly, offered no comment.

No hard frost in three weeks. That's what the morning weatherman said.

Another governor says this is a time of reflection and prayer. He says everyone should go to church. Then he says he means "house of worship."

A wren is dancing on my neighbor's No Trespassing sign.

"Design thinking" is this week's newsworthy phrase.

Tomorrow I'll take out the tiller for the small, annual work it does. Some years I still find arrowheads. Other years it's just red dirt, rocks, and worms.

Hitchhiking Towards the Apocalypse

I sat on a rock beside a four lane highway.
The Sunday sun kept me company.
Occasionally, the wind stopped by.

My shirt was faded blue denim.
If my shirt was pond water, the fish could see me.

I had a black-and-white postcard in my shirt pocket.
Every few minutes,
I'd take it out, squint, and pretend it was more than one place.

Unfinished Poem

Here are desires, cave deep
Here is the man and woman who kiss secrets on your bed,
While every light burns in the house
Here is the dream of the butterfly tattoo and the red shoe box of letters
Here is dust shaken off as an offering on your doorstep
Here is part of the river you always carry
Here is one piece to a child's puzzle
The puzzle piece resembles a mountain or an ocean seen far off
Here is the sound of skipping rope
Here are dandelions, fresh from the ditch's edge

The Man in the Yellow Hat

The man in the yellow hat is gone. He was barely here. They say that about spring in Maine. Then the three days of summer arrive with beetles, bears, and tourists. And who is there to celebrate warmth and cloud breaks with? Not the man in the yellow hat. Let's call him the man with no name who happens to have a big, house paint yellow hat. And let's not forget his pet monkey on a rhinestone leash. Let's at least remember the rhinestones. They would come in handy if we ever played Hansel and Gretel in the forest. We could take turns being the witch. On the right day, we could forget the way home.

So Far Away From Tuscany

The day my father taught me how to apply makeup was an important day. Mother too busy chopping wood and practicing her tremulous falsetto. Don't we all have some story to tell? The first bit of astronomy I learned was the location of Venus in the night sky. Sit outside long enough, you'll assign value to whatever you can't reach. Such comforts are important during late night walks and barroom ruinations. No one ever told me to whistle while I work. So I seldom carry a tune more than three daylight steps. That's far enough to impersonate joy. We don't have to be always clowns even if our makeup is badly done. And we can still juggle as if we are. Sometimes shadows might be our audience.

A Slow, Secret Life

Before I began this life, I took a correspondence course
In tiny house repair. Nothing was remembered after a certificate
Was granted. Memory, always the hardest game to play.
My friend, Joe, complains more about it each year. He has
Aged, immeasurably, with sunspots and wisdom, like almost everyone.
I have remained a little girl, thighs powdered white, mimicking
My grandmother's red lipstick poses. Despite it all, my weight
Varies depending on how broken the scale. Possibly every
Wish I've ever made has been over a chocolate bar.
I've met many angels in my most secret life. Each danced
The tango on the head of a needle and dropped rose stems
From their teeth along the way. And there was the time
I met Eileen Myles and loved her, but barely stuttered
More than hello. She gave a hug for knowing who
Jim Brodey was. What I know is small and particular.
My belief system, based on a combination of
Eccentric astrology and traditional Thai spices.
My heart is large, but irregular. Every friend knows when
I miss a beat. So I press leaves in pages of books,
Not yet read, as a reminder that right words are living things.
I somehow never lost my southern accent. Like my voice,
It only deepened with age. People say, I look nothing
Like my pictures. And I sound nothing like the voice
Imagined from a picture frame. It was always like this.
Even when very young and completely hidden behind
The back yard bird bath. That crinkled photo of where I first
Thought to fly. The birdbath always attracted sparrows,
Wrens, and blue jays. They sprinkled me when they bathed.

Away From the Spotlight, in the July Sun

In those days, my pockets only held lint and lottery tickets.
Goodbye to You was my theme song, hummed for at least
One hour a day. My love life based on statistics
And poor math skills. At the time, I was addicted to
Epiphanies. I found them harder to give up than
Exploding cigars. I was already carrying a
Dictionary of clichés as a ready-to-use repository
For that moment when original thought
Became too much. Even then the world was
Spinning that way. The calendar told us, along with
What was left of the news. The latest gossip always came from
Street corners and park benches. On Sunday afternoons I would
Stroll the boulevards in my faux pearl necklace with my hair
Braided into a curlicue. Most conversations were
Punctuated by sighs. I supported the idea that a person's
Net worth should be measured by the vowels in her name.
A petition to make that a law went nowhere fast or slow.
Most of my writing paper was leftover invoices. I used
Big old capitalist letters, in block print. I never used cursive
For fear my words would snake into places I didn't recognize
At first glance, which is often the only glance I want to give.
I only wrote in ocean-blue ink with a flamingo feathered pen.
It reminded me romance is possible on some beaches on any day.

Bright Red Calendar Marks

Yesterday was nothing like Easter.
Nothing like Tuesday, which is more recent.
It's easy to be silly, especially if you are a drunk juggler
With no cares about what's missed.
All the jugglers I know are retired or (worse) always sober.
I hope those aren't the only dishes I'm left with.
There's a chance any one of us
Will end with only dreams to serve.
Let me tell you about a dream wish:
When I was a child, John Wayne and Paul Lynde
Took turns watching my crib.
No wolves were ever allowed in.
As a young man, I chopped the crib for firewood.
As it burned, I danced the robot and called it a jig.
What I know of my whole story is somewhere on a
Street corner gathering cold.
There's so little I know.
Who I've met, loved, buried or walked away from
Make not-so-different lists.
So little variety to blush about.
Nothing as exciting as bathroom graffiti.
Not even much compared to overheard remarks
On park walks in spring.

About the Author

Mike James makes his home outside Nashville, Tennessee. His poetry is widely published. He has read and performed his work at universities and performance venues throughout the country. His many poetry collections include: *Leftover Distances* (Luchador), *Jumping Drawbridges in Technicolor* (Blue Horse), *Crows in the Jukebox* (Bottom Dog) and *Peddler's Blues* (Main Street Rag.) He has served as an associate editor for *Kentucky Review* and *Unbroken*.

www.ingramcontent.com/pod-product-compliance
Lightning Source LLC
Chambersburg PA
CBHW021012090426
42738CB00007B/766